sport snaps
paul harris

Brendan Shanahan

the power forward

14

This book is dedicated to Charlie L. Harris and the late Ellen R. Harris. They didn't start out with a lot of material wealth, but they gave their children gifts that are far more valuable.

P.H.

PHOTO CREDITS:

Printed by Pinnacle Press, Inc. in the United States of America.

Edited by Tami Lent.

Designed by Werremeyer | Floresca.

LIBRARY OF CONGRESS CATALOG CARD NUMBER 00-100072

table of contents

the day

BRENDAN SHANAHAN WILL NEVER FORGET

the power forward

Ask any hockey player and he'll tell you that it's all about winning the Stanley Cup.

After the Red Wings had completed their four-game sweep of the Philadelphia Flyers with a 2-1 victory at Joe Louis Arena on June 7, 1997, Brendan Shanahan finally hoisted the Stanley Cup—and fulfilled his childhood dream.

"Seeing the clock tick down to zero and being handed the Stanley Cup was a real sense of accomplishment and a sense of relief," said Shanahan. "When you're playing as a kid, you wonder whether you'll ever have the chance [to win the Cup]."

Shanahan remembers seeing a photo of linemate Darren McCarty and him. Both were yelling instructions to each other on a face-off during the final game of the championship. He couldn't believe the intense expressions on their faces and was curious as to when this intensity had occurred. To his surprise, he found out that it was the last face-off of the game, with just six seconds remaining.

Shanahan was one of the final pieces that the Red Wings needed to win the Stanley Cup. It's likely his thoughts drifted to his father—who died of Alzheimer's during the summer after Shanahan's third NHL season—while lifting the Cup in victory.

BRENDAN SHANAHAN

profile

14

BORN:
JAN. 23, 1969,
MIMICO, ONTARIO

FAMILY:
WIFE, CATHERINE

IS HE A NET BOY? Definitely. Like many NHL players, Shanahan surfs the web at every opportunity.

PERSON THAT MOST INFLUENCED HIM: His father, Donal. To this day, during the playing of the national anthem before each game, Shanahan asks his father to watch over him and let him play his best.

FAVORITE BOOKS: *The Hobbit* by J.R.R. Tolkien and *Trinity* by Leon Uris.

FAVORITE AUTHOR: Leon Uris, who writes fiction based on real people and real events.

FAVORITE OFF-SEASON RECREATION: Getting away to his Ontario cottage, which is located north of Toronto.

WHAT HE WOULD HAVE DONE HAD HE NOT PLAYED HOCKEY: Shanahan is a voracious reader on varied subjects and is a natural storyteller himself. One could see him as anything from a college professor to a stand-up comedian to an actor.

SPECIAL INTEREST: Shanahan currently does work with the Alzheimer Society of Canada. The main event he sponsors is the annual Alzheimer Coffee Break, which raises about one million dollars per year. During the month of September, money is donated to the Alzheimer Society whenever coffee is purchased at bagel shops, donut shops or wherever coffee can be bought in Canada. He's been involved with this event for the last four years.

WHAT HE WANTS TO ACCOMPLISH: Shanahan did not graduate from high school. After completing grade 12 (the Canadian school system goes to grade 13), he began his rookie year in the NHL. Shanahan says he would like to get his high school diploma or a GED in the future.

LATE IN THE SECOND OVERTIME OF GAME 4 OF THE 1997 WESTERN CONFERENCE SEMIFINALS, BRENDAN SHANAHAN STOOD AT THE LIP OF THE ANAHEIM CREASE AND BATTLED A MIGHTY DUCKS DEFENSEMAN.

WHEN A REBOUND SUDDENLY SPURTED OFF THE PADS OF DUCKS GOAL-TENDER MIKHAIL SHTALENKOV, SHANAHAN SHOVED THE DEFENSEMAN OUT OF THE WAY, SQUARED UP TO THE NET AND SNAPPED A SHOT INTO THE YAWNING OPENING TO END THE GAME AND THE SERIES AND SEND THE DETROIT RED WINGS INTO THE WESTERN CONFERENCE FINALS.

NHL | career playoff goals scored: 37

Red Wings fans had long dreamed about this kind of victory. And with Shanahan playing a key role, Detroit went on to win the first of two-straight Stanley Cups.

The 6-foot-3-inch, 218-pound Shanahan can play the game of hockey any way he wants. He's skilled enough to have recorded four seasons of 40-plus goals (twice he's scored more than 50 goals); he's tough enough to have collected over 100 penalty minutes in every one of his 12 NHL seasons going into the 1999-2000 season; and he's good enough defensively to kill penalties.

"I love this guy," said current Boston Bruins coach Pat Burns, who's the former coach of the Montreal Canadiens and Toronto Maple Leafs. "He does it all: scores, fights, hits, checks. He's a great player."

But Shanahan wasn't always that well-rounded of a player. After the New Jersey Devils had made him the second-overall pick in the 1987 NHL Entry Draft, Shanahan was admittedly over his head as an 18-year-old rookie. He literally fought his way to respect as he challenged most of the NHL's heavyweight brawlers. He scored only seven goals and 19 assists in 65 games as a Devils rookie in 1987-88, but he also had 131 penalty minutes.

"I'm not ashamed to say it, I was in over my head when I first came into the league," Shanahan said. "My first [fight] was against Jay Wells, and I remember the team got a boost from it, guys patted me on the back after the game. It was respect."

Shanahan continually improved; he picked up pointers from teammates and developed into an all-around force. Probably the biggest improvement he has made over the years is learning how to get into shooting position to deliver one of the best one-time slap shots in the National Hockey League. It's a skill that Shanahan learned from Brett Hull when they served together as St. Louis Blues teammates. "Watching Hullie from the minute he crosses the blue line, he puts himself in a position to shoot," said Shanahan. "The puck never surprises him."

Not only has Shanahan endeared himself to teammates over the years, but he is also a favorite among the people who cover the NHL. For most of his career, Shanahan has enjoyed talking to the media and is one of the "go-to guys" for reporters. His comments are insightful, different and entertaining—even if all of his stories about his summer activities aren't purely factual.

"You guys are going to love him. He speaks from the heart," said then-Hartford Whalers coach Paul Holmgren to the beat writers who covered the Whalers in Shanahan's first training camp with Hartford in September 1995.

Shanahan's physical presence has continued to be a big part of his game. Even when he posted successive 50-goal seasons for the Blues in 1992-93 and 1993-94, Shanahan has never hesitated to drop his gloves. "It's my nature," he said. "I've grown up enough to know that you don't do it off the ice, but within the sport [fighting] happens. I don't like to think about it because, if I do, it's nerve-wracking. But I enjoy it every once in a while."

Given his background (he's the youngest of four boys) and his size, it isn't a surprise that Shanahan matured into a rough-and-tumble hockey player who doesn't mind fighting one bit. In all likelihood, his father's working-class background has a lot to do with the way Shanahan plays the game as well.

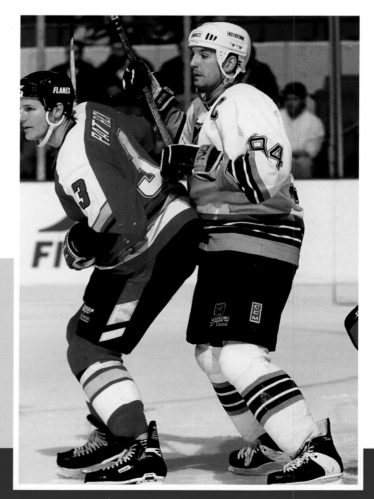

Irish-Canadian immigrant Donal Shanahan was a man who did whatever it took to take care of his family. After he arrived in the Toronto area and met his future wife, Rose, who had also recently immigrated from Ireland, Donal moonlighted as a gravedigger while putting himself through firefighting school. He and Rose went on to raise a middle-class family of four boys: Don, Brian, Shaun and Brendan.

The Shanahan boys liked to play—and play hard. Of course, that play led to fights between the brothers most of the time. Brendan is 11 years younger than Don, eight years younger than Brian and six years younger than Shaun. Naturally, Brendan got the worst of things in the early days.

"This is a guy who fills a very vital role on the team,
a guy who takes the pressure off the guys around him and makes everybody else better."

PAUL HOLMGREN, FORMER HARTFORD WHALERS COACH

But while the Shanahan boys battered each other, no one from outside of the family was allowed to touch any of them. If that happened, the unfortunate interloper would have to deal with all four Shanahan brothers.

Not only did Brendan have to fight his older siblings, but Shaun often played matchmaker for his youngest brother. He directed Brendan to fight those kids in school whom Shaun felt were too young for him to fight himself. "It was like living with Don King," Brendan said.

NHL | career playoff games played: 101

101

One of Brendan's fondest memories was of watching his brothers play Junior A lacrosse. "I loved the camaraderie they had," he said. "If one guy got into a fight, it would only take a minute until the other one was fighting. No one wanted to be outdone."

At the age of 15, Brendan played Tier II Junior hockey with Mississauga of the Metropolitan Toronto Hockey League. He used his skill and strength to record 20 goals and 21 assists for 41 points in 36 games. At that level, he was so physically superior to most of his opponents that it wasn't necessary for him to take penalties or fight that often. He had only 26 penalty minutes.

Off the ice, Brendan loved spending time with Donal. When he would take Brendan to early-morning practice, Donal would bring his pipe and a rolled-up copy of the *Toronto Star*. He would encourage all of the young players by tapping them with his paper. Because of this, Brendan's teammates called Donal "Father Don."

NHL | career playoff assists: 44

forty-four

Around the time Brendan was in the ninth grade, Donal began to change. The father that Brendan idolized began forgetting things, driving erratically and becoming confused. Donal was suffering with the first stages of Alzheimer's disease. When the Shanahans took a family trip to Ireland the summer that Brendan was 16, Donal sometimes couldn't even remember his youngest son's name.

Despite that personal tragedy, Brendan continued his hockey career.

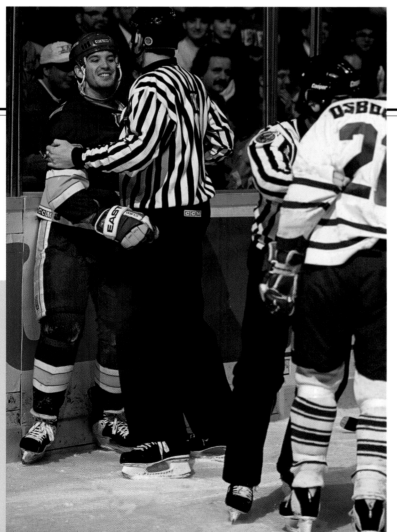

Shanahan moved on to the London Knights of the Ontario Hockey League after the family returned from Ireland in the fall. He had a good rookie season, scoring 28 goals and 34 assists in 59 games. He also had 70 penalty minutes.

His performance drew the eye of NHL scouts, who really took notice the following season. In just 56 games, Shanahan scored 39 goals and 53 assists and had 92 penalty minutes. He also served as a member of Team Canada for the World Junior Championships in Piestany, Czechoslovakia, that same year. In six games, Shanahan had three goals and four assists for seven points.

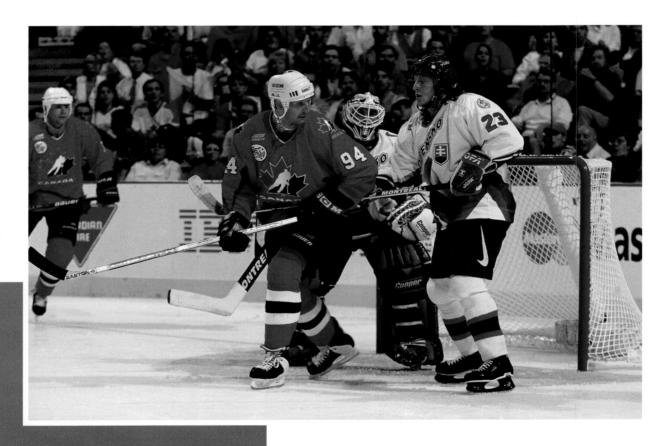

"I guess the closest word to describe him is 'power' forward.

He's going to score big goals and he's going to check and he'll fight. He brings a lot when he's playing well."

DAVE LEWIS, RED WINGS ASSOCIATE COACH

The 1987 NHL Entry Draft was scheduled to be at Detroit's Joe Louis Arena; Shanahan was one of the top prospects. The Buffalo Sabres had the first pick of the draft and took center Pierre Turgeon. The New Jersey Devils had the next pick, and they selected Shanahan.

About two hours into the drive back home from Detroit, Donal asked an old friend of Brendan's, who had accompanied the family to the draft, "Who was that back there?" But after a little while, Donal said, "I was very proud of that boy back there."

At the age of 18, Brendan Shanahan was about to realize one of his dreams: playing in the National Hockey League.

NHL | **second player selected in 1987 NHL Entry Draft**

AS AN 18-YEAR-OLD NEW JERSEY DEVILS ROOKIE DURING THE 1987-88 SEASON, 6-FOOT-3-INCH SHANAHAN WAS CERTAINLY BIG, STRONG AND TOUGH AT 210 POUNDS. BUT HE WAS QUITE GREEN WHEN IT CAME TO PLAYING THE GAME AT THE NHL LEVEL.

915

NHL | career games played: 915

In short, Shanahan wasn't experienced enough to anticipate the play and wasn't fast enough to keep up. He relied on his fists and toughness and took on all comers in fisticuffs. Not only did he earn the respect of his teammates with his courage, but, on many occasions, his fights gave the Devils a needed boost in games.

Shanahan finished his rookie season with only seven goals and 19 assists for 26 points. In 65 games, he had 131 penalty minutes. But he helped the Devils to the franchise's first playoff berth since the 1977-78 season.

New Jersey made it into the playoffs with an overtime victory over the Chicago Blackhawks in the last game of the season. The unlikely Devils then advanced to the Wales Conference finals, where they were defeated by the Boston Bruins in seven games.

While Shanahan struggled as a rookie, the rink was the only place he felt comfortable. That's not surprising when one considers that he was a teenager alone in an unfamiliar place.

Shanahan was also missing the opportunity to complete his final year of high school and graduate with his classmates. His rookie season in the NHL would have been his senior year in high school (grade 13 in Canadian schools). But, because he was pursuing his profession and dream, he didn't graduate from high school. Shanahan discovered he missed attending school and having his brain challenged in a classroom environment. "I really actually enjoyed high school," he said. "I ran out of time." In fact, after his second NHL season, Shanahan said he took a class during the summer because he was bored.

NHL | career points: 846

846

And the fact that he was so much younger than the rest of his teammates took something away from one of the most memorable moments of any NHL skater: scoring that first goal.

After Shanahan had beaten an NHL goaltender for the first time, he planned to celebrate with his teammates by footing the beverage bill at a postgame gathering at a local establishment. When he arrived at the gathering place, he wasn't allowed inside because he was only 18. "I wound up handing in my money from outside the door, and I went home while my teammates drank on me," he said.

Shanahan's second season began even more slowly, statistically speaking, than the first had. Through the first 40 games, he remembers having only about 10 points. He was becoming frustrated that his game wasn't developing sufficiently.

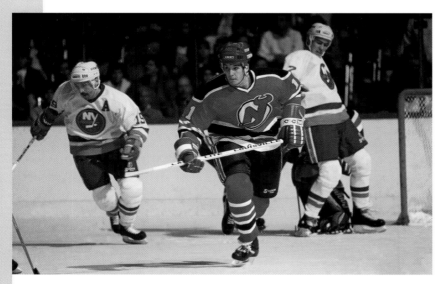

Midway through the second season, however, he got a break.

New Jersey forward Mark Johnson suffered an injury and was forced out of the line-up. Among the moves Devils coach Jim Schoenfeld made to compensate for Johnson's injury was making Shanahan the left wing on a line with center Patrik Sundstrom and right wing John MacLean. In junior hockey and to that point in his NHL career, Shanahan had played right wing and center.

Despite Shanahan's position switch, the unit clicked immediately. Shanahan had four points in his first game with Sundstrom and MacLean. In fact, he equaled the 10 points he had collected in the season's entire first half in the first 10 games the line was together.

IF YOU ARE A DEFENSEMAN FACING AN
ONCOMING PLAYER WHO HAS THE PUCK,
KEEP YOUR EYES ON HIS CHEST AND/OR
STOMACH AREA. HE HAS TO GO WHERE
HIS TRUNK IS GOING. DON'T LOOK AT
THE PUCK AND DON'T LOOK IN HIS EYES.
IF YOU DO, YOU MAY GIVE UP A GOAL.

#1

Sundstrom was a skilled playmaker while MacLean was the line's sniper. Shanahan added the physical element of digging for the puck in the corners and going to the net to create traffic, tip in shots and put in rebounds.

"Most of my goals and points came from driving to the net and one of those guys shooting it in off my leg or something," said Shanahan.

"He's studied the game well.
The talent was always there, but it was just the case of
him figuring stuff out.
He's **figured it out.**"

PAT VERBEEK, RED WINGS FORWARD AND FORMER NEW JERSEY DEVILS TEAMMATE

Not only were Sundstrom and MacLean talented, but they were both smart players who shared their knowledge with Shanahan. "Whenever I got off the ice, those guys would be talking about what I did right or wrong," he said. "Playing with those guys gave me the kick I needed to learn the game."

In the following 1989-90 season, Shanahan began to be the dominant NHL power forward that he is today. He reached the 30-goal mark and had 42 assists for 72 points. He also had 137 penalty minutes.

NHL | career goals scored: 420

420

Soon after, Shanahan began to emulate one of his idols, Tim Kerr. Kerr had scored over 50 goals in four-straight seasons with the Philadelphia Flyers from 1983-84 until 1986-87. A center and right wing, he was about the same size and build as Shanahan. "Kerr was just a big, strong guy who was immovable [in front of the net]," said Shanahan. "I've got a great big rear end that was unmovable. If I can keep my balance and get my rear end in somebody's chest, I'm O.K."

But as Shanahan began to come into his own as an NHL player, Donal's condition was quickly deteriorating.

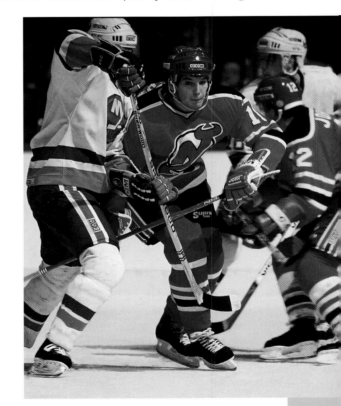

When the Devils played a game in Buffalo during Shanahan's third season, his family went to New York to watch him play. What Shanahan didn't know was that it was thought his father had approximately one week to live. Rose Shanahan told New Jersey general manager Lou Lamoriello about her husband's condition before the game. She asked that Brendan not be told until after the match.

"So after the game I was told, 'You're not going to complete the trip with your teammates. You're going back home to be with your father,'" remembered Shanahan.

> "One of the few guys in the league who can play the game different ways. I know from playing against him. **He can beat you with his size, he can beat you with his skill, he can score goals from in tight** and he's got a good enough shot that he can beat you from farther out."
>
> MARK HOWE, RED WINGS SCOUT AND FORMER NHL PLAYER

Donal rallied and held on to life for a while longer, but he finally succumbed to Alzheimer's the following summer.

Shanahan came back in the 1990-91 season with an effort of 29 goals and 37 assists for 66 points. In 75 games, he had 141 penalty minutes. While things were developing quite well for him on the ice, off the ice things weren't so great.

Lou Lamoriello is one of the toughest negotiators in the NHL and the Devils one of the most frugal organizations. After Shanahan had played out the life of his original contract with New Jersey, he signed a free-agent contract with the St. Louis Blues on June 25, 1991.

Shanahan was ready to blossom as a legitimate NHL superstar.

He was also about to enter a love affair with the city of St. Louis and its die-hard Blues fans.

ALTHOUGH THE BLUES HAD SIGNED SHANAHAN AS A FREE AGENT, AN ARBITRATOR HAD RULED THAT ST. LOUIS HAD TO SEND DEFENSEMAN SCOTT STEVENS TO NEW JERSEY AS COMPENSATION FOR SHANAHAN. SHANAHAN, HOWEVER, QUICKLY WON OVER THE CITY WITH HIS TALENT, WORK ETHIC, TOUGHNESS AND PERSONALITY. HE SCORED—UP TO THAT POINT—A CAREER-HIGH 33 GOALS. HE ALSO HAD 36 ASSISTS FOR 69 POINTS IN 80 GAMES. HE COLLECTED A CAREER-HIGH—ALSO UP TO THAT POINT—171 PENALTY MINUTES DURING THE 1991-92 SEASON.

102

NHL | single-season most points: 102

Off the ice, Shanahan organized a celebrity softball game to raise money for Alzheimer's research and to honor his father. He talked about how devastating the disease is to the family of someone who has it. "It's a horrible disease for the family," he said, recalling his own family's experience. "First, he [the person with Alzheimer's] is calling you by your brother's name. Then he's calling you by his brother's name and, eventually, not calling you by any name at all. Finally, he's not even knowing who you are."

But the people of St. Louis were certainly finding out who Brendan Shanahan was. Single at the time, and with his matinee idol good looks, he became a local celebrity. He made it his business to get out and mingle with St. Louisans and find out more about them and their city.

He also continued his effort to learn on the ice.

Brett Hull, one of the greatest pure goal scorers in the history of the NHL, served as one of Shanahan's teammates. In the three-year stretch from 1989-90 to 1991-92, Hull scored 228 goals. He scored many of his goals from the perimeter with a shot that was hard and amazingly fast. He had perfected the one-timer (when a player doesn't stop the puck before shooting as he receives a pass) off the snap shot and slap shot.

His success wasn't lost on Shanahan, who worked with Hull and developed his own deadly one-timer from the perimeter.

He also learned from Hull how to get open for those one-timers. "The trick to being open is never being in the right spot too early and Hullie is great at that," said Shanahan. "There's a time to make noise, to barge in front of the net and there's a time to get there quietly."

"He wants guys to push themselves because he pushes himself.
He'll grab you by the hair and kick you in the rear when you need it."

KELLY CHASE, FORMER ST. LOUIS BLUES AND HARTFORD WHALERS TEAMMATE

But the results of those lessons were anything but quiet for Shanahan. In 1992-93, he reached the golden 50-goal plateau with 51 goals and 43 assists for 94 points. And he still continued to play a physical game, as his 174 penalty minutes would attest. With that performance, he joined the likes of Boston Bruin Cam Neely, Pittsburgh Penguin Kevin Stevens and Calgary Flame Gary Roberts as the NHL's top power forwards.

He also found the balance between being a scorer and being a physical presence.

fifty-two

NHL | single-season most goals: 52

"In the past, if I scored a goal and we still lost, I would be told I wasn't physical enough," said Shanahan late in the 1992-93 season. "Then, if I got into a fight and threw some hits and we lost, I was told I wasn't thinking enough about offense. Now I don't drive home and bang my head against the wall thinking about it."

While he was still physical, he didn't fight as much as he had previously. He had collected 10 fighting majors in 1991-92, but he had only one in 1992-93.

The following season Shanahan accomplished the power forward's triple crown: 50 goals, 100 points and 200 penalty minutes. He had 52 goals, 50 assists and 211 penalty minutes, an achievement which led to him being named an NHL First Team All-Star at the end of the season.

"He's really grown," said Bob Berry, who coached the Blues during the 1992-93 and 1993-94 seasons. "Not only with what he's produced on the ice, but also the influence he's had in the dressing room. He's become a leader in there."

Shanahan also became legendary for the fictitious answers he provided for the Blues media guide on his off-season activities. According to Shanahan, he had lived in an Irish manor, had run with the bulls in Pamplona, had auditioned for the role of Dino in "The Flintstones" movie, was a backup goaltender for Ireland in soccer's World Cup, had served as a ball boy in an Andre Agassi match at the U.S. Open, was an extra in the football scene in "Forrest Gump" and had played saxophone at a jazz festival.

On the serious side of things, labor difficulties between the NHL owners and the NHL Players' Association led to a lockout, which shrank the 1994-95 season to 48 games. That wasn't the only big change for the Blues and Shanahan. Mike Keenan, who had led the New York Rangers to the 1994 Stanley Cup, had been hired as the Blues coach and general manager.

It was assumed that Shanahan would be the type of player whom Keenan, a tough and demanding coach, would love. Early in his tenure, Keenan spoke glowingly of Shanahan. "He can adapt his game in several ways," said Keenan. "He's proven to be a goal scorer. And the biggest thing that he brings in terms of his personal attributes are his size and strength and his competitiveness. He's a fiery player."

NHL | scored two goals in 1994 All-Star Game

two

But, for whatever reason, the honeymoon wouldn't last long between Shanahan and his new coach. Many people close to the situation speculated that Keenan didn't want a player on his team as popular with the fans as Shanahan was.

Despite the friction between the two, no one in the league—least of all Shanahan—was prepared for the June 27, 1995, deal in which Keenan sent Shanahan to the Hartford Whalers for defenseman Chris Pronger. Pronger, who had only two seasons under his belt, hadn't come close to being the dominant player he has since become.

Shanahan got the word he had been dealt when he was in a Manhattan, N.Y., restaurant doing a photo shoot with several other NHL players. "I was in shock," said Shanahan, after Keenan had told him over the phone he had been traded. "I went back to the table (which also included NHL commissioner Gary Bettman) and told them I was traded and I left. I went back to the hotel."

Shanahan said he stayed awake most of the night thinking about how big a part of his life St. Louis had become and how things were going to change. "I felt real loneliness," he said. "The big thing was, I came to St. Louis by myself as a 22-year-old kid. I grew up here. I feel I built something here, but now I'm leaving with nothing but what I'm carrying on my back."

He added: "I'm not known just as a hockey player [in St. Louis]. I'm someone people see at the grocery store, or out at dinner or out in the community, or at charity events. I like the fact that I'm not known as Brendan Shanahan. I'm known as 'Shanny.' It makes me feel like they're my friends and family."

The fact that he was going to Hartford compounded his sadness. The Whalers were one of the NHL's worst teams and had been experiencing serious financial problems.

Two days after the trade, Hartford general manager Jim Rutherford and coach Paul Holmgren took Shanahan to lunch and offered him the role of team captain. Shanahan told them he was flattered by the offer, but he wanted to talk to his new teammates before making a decision.

He also immediately shot down the idea of the Whalers unretiring John McKenzie's No. 19 (the number Shanahan had worn with the Blues) and chose No. 94, the number he had worn for Team Canada in the 1994 World Championships. After checking things out with the players during training camp, Shanahan accepted his team's captaincy on October 6, 1995.

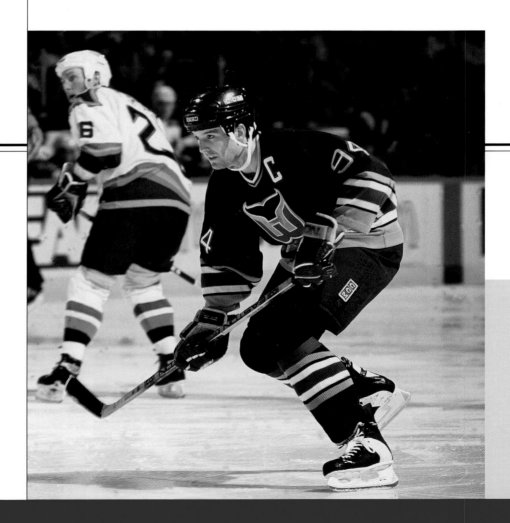

The Whalers, however, continued to struggle and missed the playoffs. Despite an early-season sprained wrist that forced him to miss eight games and hampered him for much of the season, Shanahan still managed 44 goals and 34 assists for 78 points. In 74 games, he had 125 penalty minutes.

Both Shanahan and Whalers management came to the realization that Hartford and Shanahan weren't made for each other. With its attendance problems and financial instability (the Whalers would become the Carolina Hurricanes at the start of the 1997-98 season), the team simply couldn't afford Shanahan. And the Whalers weren't a playoff contender, so Shanahan wasn't happy.

Shanahan played on Team Canada in the 1996 World Cup of Hockey. Despite Canada finishing second to Team USA in the competition, one of Shanahan's Team Canada teammates came away impressed with him and thought Shanahan could be the ingredient his team needed to put it over the top.

Detroit Red Wing Steve Yzerman told the Red Wings management staff that Brendan Shanahan would be a good fit for their team, and—because of the power forward's situation in Hartford—the Whalers would probably be receptive to a deal.

NHL | career assists: 426

chapter four: No Panic in Detroit

On November 9, 1996, after several stops and starts and near misses on a proposed deal, Shanahan was traded to the Red Wings along with minor-league defenseman Brian Glynn for Keith Primeau, Paul Coffey and the Red Wings' first-round pick in the 1997 NHL Entry Draft.

NHL | **career hat tricks: 12**

twelve

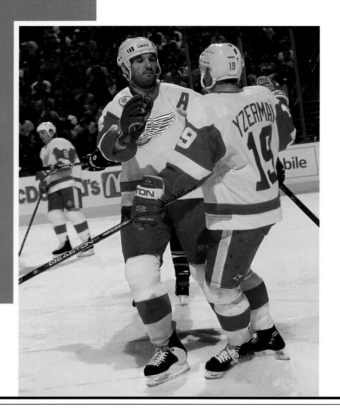

That was the day of the Red Wings' 1996-97 home opener against the Edmonton Oilers. Shanahan arrived at Detroit's Joe Louis Arena as the Red Wings were getting dressed for warm-ups. Red Wings captain Steve Yzerman instructed the rest of the players to wait until Shanahan could get dressed and hit the ice with his new teammates.

Shanahan was the power forward that Red Wings fans thought their team needed. Detroit had been one of the NHL's most talented teams since the beginning of the decade, but it had always lacked the necessary grit and size to win the Stanley Cup. The previous two seasons, the Red Wings had recorded the NHL's best regular-season record (in 1995-96, the team had even set an NHL record with 62 wins), but they hadn't been the NHL's best when it really counted.

Shanahan was the major symbol of how the Red Wings needed to retool their team to win the Stanley Cup. But, from the beginning, he downplayed his importance. "I'm just a piece of the puzzle," he said in a hastily arranged press conference after his first game as a Red Wing. "Not the only piece of the puzzle."

Shanahan also talked about how happy he was to be with an "Original Six" team. That point was driven home the following morning when he was sitting at his locker stall before practice, and Red Wings great and Hockey Hall of Fame member Ted Lindsay walked into the Red Wings dressing room.

Lindsay, who was still active with the Red Wings alumni, often worked out in the Red Wings weight room and even had a locker stall with his name above it in the dressing room. The rest of the players were accustomed to seeing the then-71-year-old Lindsay on a regular basis.

"He was something the Red Wings certainly needed. He's a winner. He would have fit in very well in the six-team league."

TED LINDSAY, FORMER RED WINGS GREAT AND A HALL OF FAMER

But it was something new and exciting for Shanahan. "I look up and there's 'Terrible Ted' (Lindsay's nickname during his playing days)," said Shanahan. "To be a left wing and see one of the greatest left wings of all time in the same room, that's something else."

Shanahan took care of business on the ice. He wound up the season as the Red Wings' leading scorer with 88 points and leading goal producer with 47 goals, including the 300th of his NHL career early in the season. And shortly after he had arrived in Detroit, he took on two of the NHL's heavyweights in fights: San Jose Shark Marty McSorley and Chicago Blackhawk Bob Probert.

Shanahan also dove headlong into Detroit's rivalry with the Colorado Avalanche. During a bench-clearing brawl in a game between the two teams at Joe Louis Arena on March 26, 1997, Shanahan executed a head-first flying leap to intercept Avalanche goaltender Patrick Roy as he tried to come to the aid of another Colorado player.

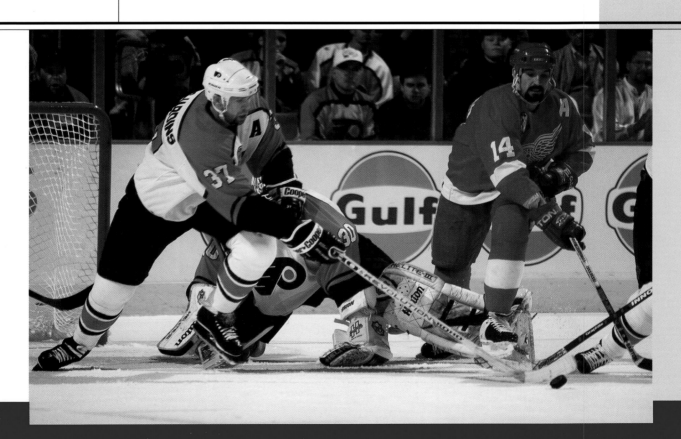

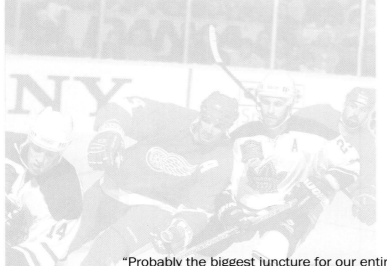

Red Wings players credited that contest with making them a team and setting the stage for the 1997 Stanley Cup run. Detroit rallied from a 5-3 third-period deficit. Shanahan scored the tying goal and assisted on Darren McCarty's overtime game-winner.

"Probably the biggest juncture for our entire team," said Shanahan about the game against the Avalanche. "That was like a war. Not just a war of fatigue. We hadn't beaten them since the playoffs the year before," he remarked, referring to Colorado's Western Conference playoff win over the Red Wings.

That contest also began Shanahan's own personal battle within the Red Wings-Avalanche rivalry.

After Shanahan's dive to intercept Roy, Colorado's tough and physical defenseman Adam Foote rushed to aid his goaltender. As hockey goaltender etiquette demands, Red Wings goaltender Mike Vernon immediately bolted into the fray from the other end of the ice as soon as Roy moved to get involved. He paired off with Roy—and Shanahan and Foote began to pummel each other. The tough, physical play between Shanahan and Foote would continue throughout the next few seasons in games between the two teams.

NHL | **tied for first in power-play goals in 1997**

Although the Red Wings finished the season with the third-best record in the NHL's Western Conference, they defeated the St. Louis Blues, Anaheim Mighty Ducks and Colorado Avalanche in the playoffs. Shanahan was responsible for ending the second-round series against Anaheim with a goal 17:03 into the second overtime of Game 4.

The Red Wings then advanced to the Stanley Cup finals against the Philadelphia Flyers. The finals were over almost as soon as they started, as the Red Wings swept the Flyers to win the franchise's first Stanley Cup since 1955. Shanahan scored twice in Game 2, a 4-2 victory over the Flyers, and added a goal and an assist in Game 3, a 6-1 win. After the Red Wings had won Game 4 to win the Cup, Shanahan was obviously ecstatic.

"We became a team during the season. It was a painful excursion at times and there were many, many bumps along the way," said Shanahan of the 1996-97 season. "But no matter where we end up, we'll always have this moment for the rest of our lives."

Shanahan remembers the last few seconds of the 2-1 victory over the Flyers at Joe Louis Arena in Game 4 to clinch the Cup.

"I looked at the clock and it was ticking down...," he said. "I turned around and I was still a little nervous a bit. But I looked and saw Steve [Yzerman] throw his stick in the air...and at that point it was just pure exhilaration."

Shanahan had accomplished what every hockey player dreams of: winning the Stanley Cup.

But just six days later, a limousine accident ended the careers of Red Wings defenseman Vladimir Konstantinov and team masseur Sergei Mnatsakanov. Both still remained in wheelchairs at the end of 1999 due to head injuries.

With the loss of Konstantinov and the trade of Vernon to the San Jose Sharks, the Red Wings weren't expected to repeat as Cup champions.

The Red Wings played well as a team throughout the season and once again finished third overall. But Shanahan's personal numbers plummeted. He finished with only 28 goals, which was his lowest total for a full season since his second NHL season.

Hockey Tips for Young Players: IMPROVING YOUR SHOT

#3

While big booming slap shots look impressive, wrist shots and snap shots wind up in the net more often. The two most important components of scoring are getting the shot away quickly and getting it on net. Focus on getting your shot away as quickly as you can and making sure it's on goal. That means you have to work on strengthening your hands, wrists and forearms. The two best ways to do this are wrist curls and the old hockey exercise of tying some kind of weight to a hockey stick; holding the stick out in front of you; turning the stick until the weight has been rolled up on the stick; and rolling the stick back down. While proper shooting technique stresses getting your legs into your shot—if you have the time to do so, this is a must—many times you can beat a goaltender with just a quick snap of your wrists while you're on the move, depending on where the shot is placed. But this can only be accomplished if your hands, wrists and forearms are sufficiently strong enough to produce a reasonably hard shot with a snap of the wrists.

Because of his scoring problem, Shanahan adjusted his style of play. "Marty [Red Wings teammate and sometimes linemate Martin Lapointe] and I kind of changed roles," he said. "I had a tough time shooting the puck. I kind of drove to the net and that opened up Marty to shoot."

There was also another disappointment for Shanahan during the 1997-98 season.

NHL players were participating in the Winter Olympics for the first time in history at the 1998 games in Nagano, Japan. Shanahan was selected to play for Team Canada.

Members of Team Canada were hopeful of a gold medal but came away with nothing to show for their efforts.

The beginning of the end was a loss to the eventual gold medal-winning Czech Republic. The game was tied after regulation time and went to a shootout. Team Canada coach Marc Crawford picked Calgary's Theoren Fleury, Dallas' Joe Nieuwendyk, Boston's Ray Bourque, Philadelphia's Eric Lindros and Shanahan to take the shots.

> " There's no bad pass to Shanny.
> Any pass anywhere near his body, he can adjust to it
> and get a shot on goal....
>
> # Any pass is a good pass and he can score on it."
>
> IGOR LARIONOV, RED WINGS TEAMMATE

Each team had five shots at scoring. The team with the most goals after five attempts would win the game. If the game was still tied, another shooter for each team would attempt shots until the tie was broken.

The Czech Republic scored on its first attempt but didn't score again. Then Buffalo's Dominik Hasek, in goal for the Czech Republic, stopped the first four Canadian shooters. It came down to Shanahan to save the day.

Before he even took the ice for his shot, Shanahan decided he would try to "deke" (skate in and create an opening by making a move close to the goaltender) instead of just unloading his hard shot at an opening. His thinking was that Hasek would expect him to shoot.

"He's a power-play guy, he kills penalties. He works the boards well. He's an important player in the locker room, too."

DAVE LEWIS, RED WINGS ASSOCIATE COACH

Once Shanahan was on the ice and was prepared to take the shot, he almost decided to go in and just rip the puck at the opening between Hasek's pads (the five hole). But he decided to stick with his original plan.

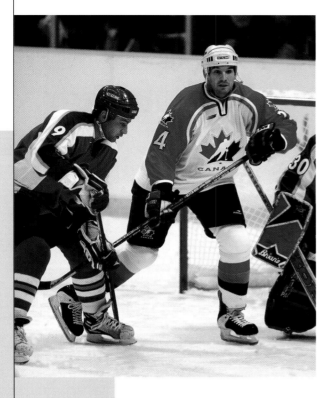

Shanahan picked up the puck, skated in on Hasek and made his move...but there was no opening.

"He came with me the whole way. I was waiting for him to commit and finally fall," Shanahan said. "He just stayed on the puck the whole way. When I shot, I knew it wasn't going in because he had everything covered. But I had to finally shoot because I would've been behind the net if I'd have waited longer."

With Canada eliminated from gold medal competition, Shanahan felt like he had choked in a big moment and let his whole country down. "It was awful. It was an awful feeling," he said. "We had such high expectations."

When he returned to the Red Wings for the last part of the season, Shanahan continued to struggle. But the Red Wings finished third overall in the Western Conference.

In the next to last game of the season against the Dallas Stars, Shanahan suffered a back injury. It wasn't serious, but he needed about two weeks of rest to completely heal. Since the Stanley Cup playoffs were about to begin, he didn't have two weeks. He missed the last game of the season and the first two playoff games but returned for Game 3 of the first-round series against the Phoenix Coyotes. He even scored a little over a minute into the game.

But his back didn't allow him to play his normal game. He did score a double-overtime goal to win Game 3 of the second-round series against the St. Louis Blues. That made him one of the few players in NHL history to have two goals in double overtime or beyond in their careers.

"The problem is, if you play him aggressively, you bring out the best in him.

But he's too good a scorer to give any room."

MARK OSBORNE, FORMER NHL PLAYER

His back really began to bother him at the start of the Western Conference finals against Dallas. "I stayed back and played the left-wing lock [the Red Wings' main defensive system at the time]. I didn't stray deep into the offensive zone," he said. "I made sure that I wouldn't have any problems recovering. Other guys were scoring and we always scored first so we were almost always ahead. I might've played a little differently had we been behind."

The Red Wings defeated the Stars in six games to advance to the Stanley Cup finals. They then swept the Washington Capitals for their second-straight Cup.

Despite his back problems and only five goals and nine points in 20 playoff games, winning the Stanley Cup was still a thrill.

"It's still so satisfying to be a part of it," Shanahan said. "In a different role. It was important to my teammates that I didn't go out [of the line-up]."

Shanahan said the entire 1997-98 season seemed out of the ordinary. "It was a strange season. The Olympics, the disruption from the break in the middle of the season," he said. "Not having Vladdy and Sergei Mnatsakanov. Just a strange year."

Though there were some whispers that many were disappointed in Shanahan's drop in numbers and questioned his commitment, the fact remained that he had been a Red Wing for two seasons and the team had won the Stanley Cup both years. Despite his drop in production, he had led the team in goals for each of the two seasons.

The 1998-99 season would be Shanahan's first in Detroit that the Red Wings didn't win the Stanley Cup. The team was eliminated in the second round of the playoffs by the Colorado Avalanche in a six-game series.

The 1998 season began with so much promise, especially for Shanahan. He had undergone a rigorous off-season training regimen in which he emphasized building stamina and flexibility instead of building muscle, and he got off to a fast start. His line, with Yzerman at center and Darren McCarty on right wing, dominated the early going. In fact, they were the only Red Wings line producing.

But McCarty got injured, which broke up the line—and Shanahan went into another prolonged slump. One of the main reasons for Shanahan's lack of production was an inexplicable power-play drought. A power-play force for most of his career, Shanahan had scored 52 power-play goals from 1995-96 until 1997-98. For the entire 1998-99 season, he had just five power-play goals.

NHL | **All-Star appearances: 6** SIX

He finished the season with 31 goals, another disappointing
year by his standards. But he still led the team in goals.
Late-season addition Wendel Clark had 32, but 28 of those
goals came with the Tampa Bay Lightning.

No one in the National Hockey League, with the exception
of Pittsburgh Penguin Jaromir Jagr, was scoring as he had
in the past. Total goals per game were at an all-time low for
the modern-day sport, and not since the 1969-70 season
had a player not reached 50 goals. Looked at in that
context, Shanahan's goal total seemed in line with what
was going on in the rest of the league. But he only had
27 assists to total 58 points, which meant that 1998-99 was
the second-straight season he had failed to reach 60 points.

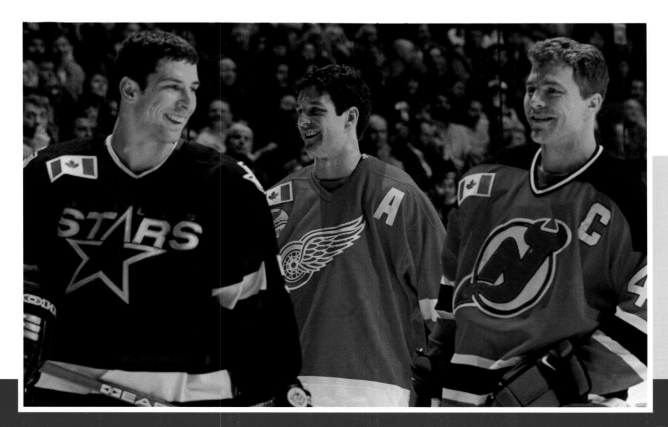

As he entered the 1999-2000 season, there were some questions about whether Shanahan would remain a Red Wing. It was the final year of his contract, and, if Detroit didn't re-sign him, he would become an unrestricted free agent on July 1, 2000. But Red Wings GM Ken Holland said that he wanted Shanahan to remain a Red Wing—and Shanahan certainly wanted to remain in Detroit.

> ❝ We don't have to convince him very much to shoot.
And when he's shooting,
he's hard to stop.
Not many guys can score from long distance
consistently, but he's one of them."

SCOTTY BOWMAN, RED WINGS COACH

Early in the 1999-2000 season,
he scored the 400th goal of his NHL
career. Coincidentally, it came against
Toronto Maple Leafs goaltender
Curtis Joseph, who had been
Shanahan's teammate with the
Blues. Shanahan was also happy that
the milestone goal came in Toronto.
His mother and three brothers were
all in attendance at the first game the
Red Wings ever played in the Maple
Leafs' brand-new Air Canada Centre.

In his fourth season as a Red Wing, Brendan Shanahan
had come to love Detroit. "When I asked for a trade
[from Hartford], I wanted to find a home," he said.
"I've found one here."

From the time Paul Maurice was promoted from assistant coach to head coach of the Hartford Whalers early in the 1995-96 season, he used Brendan Shanahan in every situation possible. He appreciated Shanahan's skill and determination, particularly the way Shanahan continued to play with a broken wrist for much of the season.

Brendan Shanahan has an outstanding ability to shoot the puck.

"He must have real strong wrists or something because he can get a shot off on a hard pass without handling it better than anybody I've ever seen...and he can get the shot off and it doesn't have to be a perfect pass."

Shanahan is an extremely physical player.

"He's a physical presence out there [on the ice] and he's got a mean streak. It probably gives him a little more room. The one or two extra feet he needs to get his shot off."

Shanahan is a leader in the locker room.

"He's one of those guys who can switch from being a practical joker and a light guy in the dressing room to his game-time face just like that."

Shanahan is a player who can play in all situations.

"You've got a safe guy on the bench. When those kind of guys are out there, you don't have to worry. There's nobody who you feel Brendan's a bad matchup against."

Shanahan is a rare combination of physical player and sniper.

"That's the one part of his game that makes him a special player. There are other guys who are just as physical and gritty as he is, but they can't shoot the puck like he can."

Shanahan is a diligent worker in practice.

"He worked hard. I think, with Brendan, he just really, really enjoys playing. He likes going to the rink and skating."

Shanahan has a great ability to play through pain.

"We got him and he broke his wrist the first game and he probably played six or seven weeks with it and still scored about eight goals. But he really struggled with it [the wrist]."

Shanahan plays his best hockey when it means the most.

"He's why we almost made the playoffs…. He scored 44 goals with a broken wrist and he just about did it in half a season because that's when he scored most of the goals."

ABOUT PAUL MAURICE

PAUL MAURICE IS THE COACH OF THE CAROLINA HURRICANES. HE BEGAN HIS NHL COACHING CAREER 10 GAMES INTO THE 1995-96 SEASON WHEN THE FRANCHISE WAS KNOWN AS THE HARTFORD WHALERS. THAT WAS SHANAHAN'S ONLY FULL SEASON IN HARTFORD. MAURICE WAS SHANAHAN'S COACH UNTIL THE LEFT WING WAS TRADED TO DETROIT EARLY IN THE 1996-97 SEASON.

MAURICE WAS ONLY 28 WHEN HE WAS PROMOTED FROM WHALERS ASSISTANT COACH TO THE TEAM'S HEAD COACH EARLY IN THE 1995-96 SEASON. THAT MADE HIM ONE OF THE YOUNGEST HEAD COACHES IN NHL HISTORY. NOW IN HIS FIFTH SEASON AS THE FRANCHISE'S HEAD COACH, MAURICE RANKS SECOND AMONG ACTIVE NHL COACHES IN CONTINUOUS SERVICE TO ONE TEAM TO DETROIT'S SCOTTY BOWMAN, WHO IS IN HIS SEVENTH SEASON WITH THE RED WINGS.

BEFORE BEING HIRED AS A HARTFORD ASSISTANT UNDER HEAD COACH PAUL HOLMGREN TO START THE 1995-96 SEASON, MAURICE HAD BEEN THE COACH AND GENERAL MANAGER OF THE DETROIT JUNIOR RED WINGS (NOW PLYMOUTH WHALERS) OF THE MAJOR JUNIOR ONTARIO HOCKEY LEAGUE DURING THE 1993-94 AND 1994-95 SEASONS. BEFORE THAT, HE HAD SERVED AS AN ASSISTANT COACH FOR THE OHL'S WINDSOR SPITFIRES AND JUNIOR WINGS AFTER HIS OWN JUNIOR CAREER WITH WINDSOR HAD ENDED BECAUSE OF AN EYE INJURY.

BORN JANUARY 30, 1967, IN SAULT STE. MARIE, ONTARIO, MAURICE; HIS WIFE, MICHELLE; AND THEIR TWO CHILDREN, SYDNEY (2) AND JAKE (1), RESIDE IN CARY, NORTH CAROLINA.

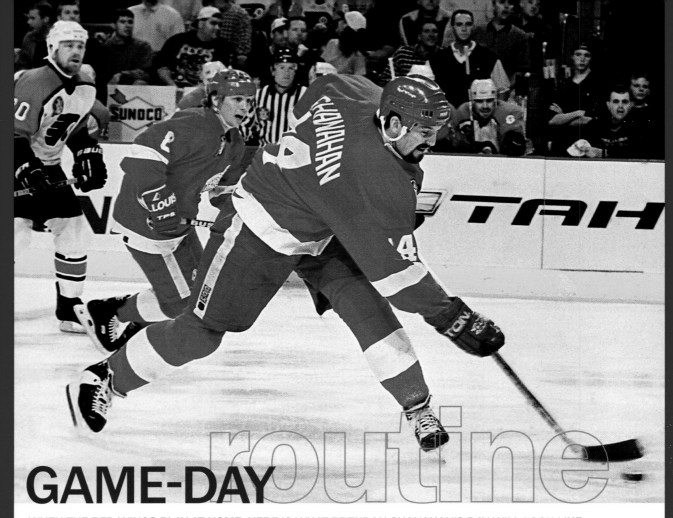

GAME-DAY routine

WHEN THE RED WINGS PLAY AT HOME, HERE IS WHAT BRENDAN SHANAHAN'S DAY WILL LOOK LIKE:

9:45 a.m.   Arrive at Joe Louis Arena for game-day skate.

10 a.m.   Get massage.

10:20 a.m.   Get dressed for skate. Most players spend more than 10 minutes dressing for a game, but Shanahan is exceptionally fast at putting on all of his equipment.

10:30 a.m.   Hit the ice for the morning skate.

10:50 a.m.   Leave the ice.

11:40 a.m.   Head home.

12:30 p.m.   Eat lunch.

2 p.m.   Take a nap.

5:30 p.m.   Arrive at Joe Louis Arena.

5:40 p.m.   Stretch, work on sticks, etc.

6:30 p.m.   Get dressed for warm-ups. Unusually superstitious, Shanahan has a routine he goes through after he gets dressed. He takes a cup of water, a cup of Gatorade and a cup of Coke and stands next to the garbage can in the dressing room. He takes a sip of each drink, spits it into the garbage can and then throws the remainder of each cup into the can. As the Red Wings head out for warm-ups, he always walks behind the player who will be his center for the game. Then one of the equipment handlers gives Shanahan his gloves, which have had the insides warmed (he repeats this before the first, second and third periods).

6:45 p.m.   Shanahan has another ritual when the team hits the ice. He circles one teammate and then touches his shoulder pads, shin pads and the ice. He circles another teammate and does the same thing. He then circles the starting goaltender in the net and repeats the ritual.

7:30 p.m.   Play game.

10:15 p.m.   Take off equipment, work out, get dressed, do postgame interviews and leave arena. The players then usually break up into groups to go out to dinner with wives and girlfriends.